POWER *of* HERE

TAJA T. HEREFORD

WestBow Press books may be ordered through booksellers or by contacting:

WestBow Press
A Division of Thomas Nelson & Zondervan
1663 Liberty Drive
Bloomington, IN 47403
www.westbowpress.com
844-714-3454

ISBN: 979-8-3850-0243-6 (sc)
ISBN: 979-8-3850-0245-0 (hc)
ISBN: 979-8-3850-0244-3 (e)

Library of Congress Control Number: 2023912974

Print information available on the last page.

WestBow Press rev. date: 07/28/2023

WESTBOW
PRESS®
A DIVISION OF THOMAS NELSON
& ZONDERVAN

This book is dedicated to my daddy, mommy, Grandma Linda, and to anyone who helped play a role in my journey from ordinary living to extraordinary purpose.

CONTENTS

FOREWORD

But he answered and said, "It is written, 'Man shall not live on bread alone,
but on every word that proceeds out of the mouth of God.'"
—Matthew 4:4 (ESV)

When Jesus spoke the previous words, he had just fasted for forty days and forty nights. He was hungry. If you have ever skipped one meal and felt the grumblings of your stomach, imagine every meal skipped for forty days and nights. Yet, Jesus did not choose to give into the devil's temptation to eat. Instead, he confronted him with the powerful words of written scripture. My father, Pastor Kenneth C. Hereford, Sr. and his wife, my mother, carried a great burden that all six of their children would be grounded in the truth of the Scriptures, and God would bless them to teach this importance to some of their grandchildren before God called my father to himself. Now that he is gone, I truly have seen the fruits of my parents' labor as all of their children have felt the call to push forward in the one and only true faith of Jesus Christ. Among these children is the author of this book, Taja Hereford. As you go through this journey, I would admonish you to do so with your Bible open. Allow the Scriptures to shape your thinking as you fast. Jesus is not only the Savior for us Christians, but he is our example. If he saw the importance of Scripture, how much more should we? We can never know Him beyond what the Scriptures have provided, and he will never contradict his word. This is good because he has not left us without answers. We can trust Him fully and wholeheartedly.

What I like most about my sister's work is that it is an encouragement to give up that which gets in the way of one's relationship with Christ. As the Bible teaches us, marriage is supposed to be a reflection of Christ and his bride the Church. Just as a faithful spouse would remove anything and everything that dares to interfere with his or her marriage, we should desire to do the same when it comes to our relationship with the Lord. Being imperfect humans at times, we forget these things, and then they tend to fester and become larger problems down the road. Sometimes it is obvious to see what is impeding upon one's relationship with Christ. If it has existed for an extended period of time and has become a regular pattern of life, it might be more difficult.

I admonish you to take true stock of your relationship with Christ and examine all the ways in which your relationship can improve.

Finally, I leave you with this. The world is becoming more evil and corrupt, but those of the true faith of Jesus Christ can stand against the evils of this world by the power of the Holy Spirit. If you take the journey presented in this book, my prayer is that you grow stronger under the conviction of the Holy Spirit through the Scriptures. The Lord will return and set this world right. Until then we, as his faithful people, must endure until the end. May you find within this journey the strength and courage the Lord offers in the Scriptures for all those who are in Him. Keep your trust in the only one who can save humankind.

Mrs. Sarchet

BACK TO THE BASICS

Here

I wish I could tell you this book was going to be some sort of life changing magic trick to help you see yourself moving from ordinary living to extraordinary purpose – seeing God in the intricate details of everything you do. However, that is not, nor will be, the case for this book. There will be no games and no gimmicks. Right now, I'm challenging you to get back to the basics. I need you to have straight up discipline in prayer, worship, Bible reading, good faith-filled community, and endurance. Now, that I've gotten that out of the way, let's talk more about what I'm hoping you will receive from this experience.

If you are or were anything like me, you might have found yourself looking for something to add some spice to your life. For me, I came to a point in my life where things seemed bleak. I was existing, but I wasn't living let alone thriving. I was going through a rough patch, some existential crisis if you will, and I needed a change. For me, it was getting back to the tenants of a good faith-filled lifestyle that would be the tools needed to change my present circumstances into a better tomorrow.

I've tried to do all the things society told me would bring me peace, happiness, and contentment. I climbed career ladders, dated around, chased a bag, and yet, still felt like I was behind the 8-ball and wasn't where I wanted to be. It wasn't until God graciously showed up through a series of unfortunate events in my life and gently whispered in my ear, "Daughter, you are right where you need to be," that I started this journey of living in my extraordinary purpose. You'll see through this experience, as you complete each activity, how God will take your current ordinary life and turn it into an extraordinary purposeful life.

You will learn how to live in the here and now while setting yourself up for a greater future filled with lives being impacted by you, circumstances turning around, and a deeper love and admiration for God. When you learn the power of being here and present with God, you will begin to see for yourself just how extraordinary your life can truly be.

What's Next?

Now is the time to get a good set of highlighters, pens, and any other office supplies to help you mark up the important pieces of information you need to learn and put in your heart. There will be sections or lessons that you might want to turn back to and repeat to deepen your understanding of that material. Certain activities will have time associated with them, but don't let yourself be constrained to the time. God does not work on time clocks, so be sensitive to the leadings of the Holy Spirit. Since your extraordinary purpose is specifically tailored to yourself, you can certainly extend activities as needed. Get ready to challenge yourself to new ways of doing things.

I'm excited to see how God turns your life around with this material. It is my hope that through my personal stories of walking through this process and the biblical connections, you too will be inspired and encouraged to go through this to see your circumstances change.

Prayer Time:

Lord, I thank you for what you are about to do in my life. I give you permission to shape me as you see fit, and I ask that you give me the grace to move this process. I trust you to take me from here to there, where I'm walking in my purpose and see the manifestation of your glory in all areas of my life. In Jesus's name, I pray, amen.

1

Position of Here

"How did you get here? Nobody's supposed to be here." These lyrics from Deborah Cox's "Nobody's Supposed to Be Here" have gone from being something I passionately sang on karaoke nights to a thoughtful question I truly started to ponder for my life. After the passing of my dad, a breakup with the love of my life, my mom going to the hospital, financial struggles from foolishly intertwining finances with my ex, taking care of children, and emotional turmoil, I literally thought I was about to lose my mind. All of this happened back-to-back, and I kept waiting for more blows to hit me out of nowhere. On the surface, it appeared that external things were just happening to me. It was hard not to want to place blame on anything or anyone outside of myself.

While going through those difficult circumstances, I asked God a powerful question that changed my whole perspective on my external situations. I asked Him, "God, what are you trying to do and show me through this?" At the time, I didn't know that God would slowly reveal multiple reasons for why I was in that position. If you are experiencing an extremely tough time in your life but haven't asked God this simple question, I would encourage you to do so now. Wait in anticipation for his responses through your journey.

God started his multipart answer with some unexpected realizations. For so long, I had allowed a good portion of my spiritual development and growth to be facilitated and piggybacked on the faith of my parents. Having grown up in a household of faith and as a pastor's kid, I received a lot of blessings from my parents, who lived out their faith and instilled it in me and my siblings. However, I am now aware that I must be autonomous and personally responsible in my own faith walk. This was a time for me to experience God in a new light. After the passing of my dad and losing his spiritual covering, I had to adopt Jesus as my father and become a daddy's girl to him. Don't get me wrong, I already knew Jesus for salvation, but I wanted to experience him in a way that was more personal. The realization of needing to experience God at another level came as I began my solemn assembly with my church. I had never done a spiritual fast before, but I needed God more than ever. I had nothing else to lose, so I took this fast seriously.

It was during this twenty-one-day fast that I started to truly hear from God. The first part of his answer to my question was the need for our relationship to be deeper. The second part really took me for a loop. I started to uncover the idolatry that I had in my heart and the self-sufficiency of thinking I was in control of my life and my world. I felt molly whopped by the convictions in my spirit as I would read my Bible, pray, fast, and listen to sermons. How could I—a pastor's kid who has been saved since I was nine years old—be so far from God in this manner?

The answer started to become clearer as I reflected over my life. Somehow, being engulfed in faith circles had convinced me that I was doing well or maintaining, because in certain areas of my life, I was fine. I didn't need to go through a big deconstruction and reconstruction of my faith because I was properly constructed by parents who knew and actively lived out being followers of Jesus. I was aware of how people could become legalistic in church, not really making it about a relationship with Jesus. I boldly stood for whom my faith was in publicly without fear of being judged. I was serving and attending church regularly, not for a checklist of Christian duties but because I knew it would fill me in my spiritual life and give worship to God. Yet I had allowed idolatry and self-sufficiency, which are branches of pride, to creep in.

When this was revealed to me, I cried. I knew I had hurt God, and I wasn't quite sure how to release these areas of my life over to Him. The practice of surrender is the hardest thing you will ever have to go through. It's picking up your cross daily and following the one who set the example for surrender (Matthew 16:24). As I continued to fast, pray, and read God's word, I became aware of the bitterness, unforgiveness, and loss of joy in my life. All of this stemmed from idolatry and self-sufficiency. This had me in a perpetual state of brokenness and sadness as I went through my fast. The emotions that come when you are convicted that something isn't pleasing to God are super humbling. These emotions didn't clear up overnight after I repented, and they did not end after my twenty-one days of fasting. It took time for God to clean up what had been developing in me because of my lack of intentionality while walking with Him. However, what took years to develop inside of me only took months to clean up when I put all the tools that helped me grow into overdrive. I'll talk about more tools later in the book, but there is a way to speed up your healing and see your circumstances turn around.

The fact of the matter was that I was indeed icky on the inside. God needed to attract my attention. Oftentimes, he does that through difficulties. When you're going through something tough, don't run from God. Go to Him because he wants to comfort you and help you become better. This is the process of sanctification. It's God's process of continuously cleaning, pruning, and tailoring people to look more like Him. When you and

I have finally come to the ends of ourselves and our solutions, we can finally open our ears and hearts toward God's thoughts and ways. God wants you in a position of humility, dependency, and brokenness so that he can continue to use you in mighty ways. In the moments when you feel low, God can reveal things to you because you are willing to let Him speak.

As I think about my story, I think about Joseph's story in Genesis 37 through 50. When Joseph was betrayed by his brothers and thrown into a pit, it was easy to blame them. Joseph had just been given two dreams about a great destiny for his life and a favoritism gift from his father. One day, Joseph was strutting in his gift, not helping his brothers work. He told them his dreams and that he would be big in life. They did not like that. His brothers took it upon themselves to teach him a lesson, and they threw Joseph in a pit to die. Don't get me wrong, what his brothers did to him was indeed evil. However, Joseph had some terrible character traits that would not be good for such a destined life as his. He lacked humility and maturity and had a lot of pride to deal with. Through the actions of others, God started his sanctification process with Joseph, preparing him for his destiny and calling. When you bring God into your mess, he can take the good, bad, and ugly and use it to benefit you in the end. God gives you this promise in Romans 8:28 (CSB), "We know that all things work together for the good of those who love God, who are called according to his purpose."

When Joseph allowed God to tailor him, God started moving Joseph toward his dreams. Though it was through a series of unfortunate events, God was weaving the story together to prepare Joseph for the calling that was specifically designed for his life. That's what God has been doing for us as well. Take some time to reflect on your life—the bad things that people have done to you, your family dynamic, and everything else—and think about how God has moved the pieces around to get you to where you are now. Did you let any negative things creep into your heart and mind that shouldn't be there? This is a good time for you to ask God to create a clean heart in you and to purify you (Psalm 51:10). The cleaning process is never fun, but when you allow God to transform you from the inside out and to change your perspective on your position in life, you will see the benefits of what you're experiencing.

The valleys of life are needed to appreciate the mountaintop moments you have. Without experiencing low moments, you wouldn't have your faith strengthened. Trials and tests are meant to show you where you are and allow you to experience God on a more intimate level. Don't let your position in the valley keep you from taking the steps necessary to move toward your destiny and make it to the mountaintop. That's the one thing you can count on from the valley—there is a guaranteed mountain waiting for you on the other side. You're responsible for the pace it takes to make it to the mountain. If you allow yourself to be distracted or give up, you will continue to delay the breakthrough that you've been wanting to experience. Don't stay in the valley; keep moving forward.

The position you're in is only necessary to help you develop. Challenge yourself to align your thoughts, attitudes, and behaviors with those of Jesus, and see how you will begin to change internally. When these situations come back around, you will be prepared to handle them as God would have you face them. He will be able to trust you with more when he can confidently see you have matured and are wiser in making your decisions. Let God determine what characteristics you need for the destiny ahead of you. Be open to the trials, challenges, and tests that will mold you into an individual who can handle an extraordinary purpose.

If you haven't been scared away yet by the idea of dealing with spiritual convictions, surrendering life's control over to God, and allowing Him to take the lead, I applaud you and cheer you on from the sidelines. As you begin the journey ahead to your extraordinary purpose, it's time to start taking some actions. The first activity will require a surrendering of physical desires to put yourself in a position to be fully submitted to God. You will be asked to complete a twenty-one-day fast. I encourage you to read the story of Joseph during the activity over the next few weeks. See what things you can glean from his example that may be useful for your process of transformation. My sincerest advice would be not to try to illegitimately shortcut this experience. You may miss things that God wants to reveal to you by trying to outrun Him in your journey. When you have finished the fast, you may proceed with the reading of this book.

Prayer Time:

Lord, I ask that you show me why you have me in this season. Help me to be receptive to the changes that you want to see in my heart, life, and character. I ask that you give me the wisdom and strength needed to move from the valley to the mountain. In Jesus's name, I pray, amen.

Position of Here Activity:

21-Day Fast
Time: 21 days

What Is a Spiritual Fast?

Society has taken pieces of a spiritual fast and adopted them to focus on the physical health benefits without adding the spiritual component to it. At the heart of a fast is the practice of giving up a desire of the flesh (physical) for the increased benefit of another aspect of life. Most of the time, people will give up food for a certain amount of time. However, with this fast, I encourage you to give up a few other things to deepen the impact and dedication to this process. In the Bible, there are many times when people or individuals completed fasts because they needed God to intervene in something major in their lives and only God could make the outcome better (e.g., Esther 4:15, Joel 1:14, Nehemiah 1:4). When you need something to change that you can't change on your own, starting with a fast will lay the foundation for God to intervene in a way you would have never seen on your own. In fact, the Bible tells us in Mark 9:29 (KJV), "And he said unto them, This kind can come forth by nothing, but by prayer and fasting." The thing you desire to see improved, restored, or bettered might only happen if you complete a fast with prayer.

Let's Begin!

Materials needed:

- Bible
- Pen
- Extra paper/prayer journal
- Notecards (optional)

5

List 2 or 3 prayer requests for this fast

Be intentional in what you choose to fast and pray over. These will be the prayer requests that you will reference throughout this journey.

_____

_____

_____

_____

This fast will take place over twenty-one days. The goal of a fast is to challenge the physical to dive into the spiritual. Therefore, I encourage you to give up something that will be difficult for you within the twenty-one days. For my twenty-one-day fast, I gave up meat, wine, and entertainment foods (e.g., sweets and snacks). List out what you will be giving up during this fast:

What I plan to give up for twenty-one days:

How to complete the fast

This is a time to increase your prayer and Bible reading time and to decrease physical gratification from outside sources. Other things you might consider giving up during this time is social media, hanging out with friends, carbs, or spending money on entertainment. Around your mealtimes, set aside time to go to God in prayer. Remember, this is a time to have God search your heart for why you are in the situation you are in. You may ask God:

- What are you trying to teach me from this situation?

- What role did I have in getting me to this place?
- Have I been following you intentionally or doing things my way?
- Search my heart for things that aren't of you and transform my mind and soul

Rhema words are those the Holy Spirit highlights for you and your situation when you are reading your Bible. When you feel the Holy Spirit speaking to you about a situation, take a notecard or write down in a prayer journal the scriptures that were spoken to you. You will need to reference these promises or affirmations along the journey. Keep these passages or scriptures somewhere that is easily accessible for you to come back and read.

During this time, God will start to reveal to you things that need to be cleaned up in you in order to prepare you for your next season. You might be dealing with unforgiveness, bitterness, idolatry, or other things that aren't good for you to continue to carry. The pruning and process of sanctification is tough. When you are confronted with the things you didn't realize were inside of you, it will be important for you to decide to keep moving forward instead of throwing in the towel. Journal your emotions using the following prompts for guidance if necessary.

- What is God showing me about myself that is not cleaned up?
- What emotions are coming up as I discover things that can be improved?
- What other resources, like counseling, might I need to help me deal with my behaviors, thoughts, and attitudes that aren't pleasing to God?

Wrap-up

Write your final thoughts as you wrap up your fast. What did you learn during these twenty-one days? Is God asking you to continue with your fast? What promises or affirmations did you receive during this time?

_____

_____

_____

_____

Process of Here

All right, how are you feeling? You're probably one month or so into this process if you're serious about seeing the change in your life that you want to see. If you have really started to take responsibility over your spiritual growth and development, you will see God starting to move in ways that you wouldn't have expected. I want you to go back and look at the prayer requests that you made during the twenty-one-day fast. Write them down in this space below so you can remind yourself what you've prayed for.

———————————————————————————————————

———————————————————————————————————

———————————————————————————————————

By now, it is my hope that you have started to see God answer these prayer requests. However, if you haven't, perhaps the reason is because you aren't familiar with how God works when it comes to getting you from *here* to *there*. I want to help you understand how God operates when it comes to answered prayers. He only has three responses: yes, no, and not yet. I, like you, would hope that God answered all my requests with a quick and fast, "Yes!" However, I would like to say for the bigger things that you really want to see, it's often a "not like that" or "not yet." These are difficult to hear, but that just means that God is working on getting you ready for your answer, getting your answer ready for you, or doing something even greater than you asked. One of the most quoted promises in the Bible relates back to this. Ephesians 3:20 (CSB) says, "Now to him who is able to do above and beyond all that we ask or think according to the power that works in us."

The good thing about God is that he does above and beyond all you ask or think. When you don't understand how he is working, you can always trust his character to see you to completion. However, it's going to be helpful for you to know how he often gets you to the answer of your prayers. After reading this chapter, go back and look at your prayer requests. See if you can start to see traces of God piecing things together in a way that may be unconventional to your way of thinking. Keep in mind Isaiah 55:8 (CSB) when it says, "For my thoughts are not your thoughts, and your ways are not my ways." When you think God is moving in an unusual way, chances are you are right! Nevertheless, he knows exactly how to connect everything together for your good.

During the fast, I asked you to look over Joseph's life in Genesis 37 through 50. He is a great example of how God took what seemed like a series of bad luck happenings and brought them together for his destiny. God works like this for multiple reasons. One reason is he likes to see if he can trust that you will be obedient to his instruction no matter what. Another reason is that he wants to make sure you are going to be a blessing to others in the interim before he blesses you. Lastly, he does that because sometimes he uses those experiences to move you to the next piece of your own destiny. God has a way of connecting seemingly random events and people to be used to catapult you in your journey.

Two notable figures who did a great job of being flexible with other assignments while on their way to bigger purposes are Paul and Jesus. Let's talk a little more about Paul first. Paul, once Saul, became a Christian and was on fire for God. The man who had been killing Christians would later become such a prominent defender of the faith that he was persecuted on behalf of it. When Paul received salvation, he knew he wanted to spread the gospel. Most importantly, he wanted to go to Rome to stand before Caesar and proclaim the good news of the gospel so that it might spread even more widely and to a new group of people. However, as Paul aimed to get to Rome, he faced a lot of trials that would take him on a unique journey to his destiny. As a prisoner, he boarded a ship that took him to Rome for his long-awaited day before Caesar. I'm sure in his mind, Paul was thinking he was finally about to see God grant him the moment he had been waiting for. Clearly, his destiny and extraordinary purpose appeared to be on the horizon. However, in Acts 27, Paul's story took an unexpected turn as the ship ran into a storm. Though Paul wanted to get to Rome, he warned the leaders of the ship that they should stay put for a few months until the season changed, and the waters would be safe enough to travel. Paul understood how this destiny thing worked. Even with Rome in the near vicinity, he still had the wisdom to know when God wanted him to take on a side job. With his advice being ignored, the entire ship was wrecked, and the people found themselves on an island called Malta (Acts 28:1–10).

In Malta, the people quickly identified Paul as someone of great spiritual authority when a snake bit him but didn't poison and kill him. The people saw him perform a miracle of healing the father of the leading man on the island. When they saw that Paul was connected to the power of God all the sick people came to him to be healed. Once Paul and the others had been there for three (3) months, it was time to set sail again. The people of Malta blessed them with all the materials they needed to get on a new ship and head for Rome. Though Paul did not expect to be shipwrecked and thrown into another project, he allowed himself to maximize the opportunity placed in front of him. Paul could have decided to grumble and not put forth his best effort in this side assignment and the results of that might have been different from the blessing he ultimately received.

Now, I want to touch on the life of Jesus. Jesus's time on earth, that's recorded for you to know, only spanned a few years. We are told about his birth. Then a story pops up when he was around twelve years old. Finally, you see what all he did from the age of thirty until his death and resurrection at thirty-three. The miracles associated with Jesus were all done over the span of three years. I could pinpoint many situations where Jesus was on his way to doing something, but never negated the opportunity to complete an additional miracle that wasn't on his original list of things to do. For example, you might be familiar with the story of the lady who couldn't stop bleeding for twelve years (Matthew 9:20–22; Mark 5:25–34; Luke 8:43–48). She reached out to touch the hem of Jesus's garment in faith, hoping that she would be healed. When she did this, she was instantly healed. However, Jesus stopped everything he was doing to publicly talk to her and to restore her.

The part of this story that I think is often overlooked is that Jesus was on his way to perform a different miracle for a man named Jairus whose daughter was dying. While Jesus was on a mission, he allowed himself to take a slight detour and delay what he was originally about to do to help someone else. If I had been Jairus, I would have been extremely confused and upset trying to hurry Jesus along instead of patiently waiting for Him to finish his encounter with the woman. However, Jesus knew that, with the slight delay, the miracle Jairus would receive would be an even greater experience than saving the daughter's life. Instead, he performed a resurrection for her, and she lived again. God knows exactly how to get the most glory from situations, even if that means rearranging the order of operations a little to complete a different task first. Don't miss out on what he wants to do through you, for you, and to you when a detour happens in your process of development.

We can pull many lessons from the examples of both Paul and Jesus. The first thing I want to reiterate is from Paul's story of his journey to Rome. While it wasn't in his ideal plan to be shipwrecked, God had more waiting for Paul to do than he even thought was a part of the blueprint for his life. If he went straight to Rome, he would have missed the greater expansion of his ministry work in Malta. Allowing yourself to be flexible and present-minded will allow God to enlarge your territory of impact. God is in the business of "Yes, and…" work. Yes, go to Rome, *and* have a revival in Malta too. Don't let your limited vision and understanding of the way God operates cause you to miss out on the bigger things he wants to do in your life.

Additionally, when you are seemingly derailed, you get to choose how you will handle that time. Will you sit there and not advance, or will you accept the challenge and make the most out of what you've been assigned? If Paul wouldn't have helped those people, who knows if the people would have eventually turned on the group of foreigners on their land. Perhaps they would have remained stranded there because they didn't have any materials to get another ship. The story could have ended in tragedy and the mission incomplete if Paul didn't understand of how God navigates our lives.

What I find interesting is that the people of Malta ended up being the resource needed to get Paul back to his original assignment. Because Paul had been faithful in his season *here* in Malta, the people of Malta helped him get *there*—to Rome. You never know how God will use the encounters you have with people or circumstances that appear unconnected to your own journey but they are actually a part of the plan. I believe so many people miss their connections to get to the next stages of their extraordinary purposes because they overlook opportunities to be blessings to others. When you miss one opportunity, God needs to get another connection for you to engage with that will propel you forward. If you don't learn the lesson about truly investing in the season you are in, God can't give you more to do.

I want to highlight one more story that demonstrates God's process of development in our current seasons and how important it is to be comfortable with a slight change of plans even when you weren't planning for it. This story revolves around David. I can't get into all the lessons to learn from David's life but take time for yourself to glean more when you can. In 1 Samuel 30, David was in a battle with the evil Amalekites. They had kidnapped all the women and children of the men soldiers when they were away, stole their possessions, and burned their town. David prayed to the Lord for guidance—a crucial step that you can't miss. The Lord told David to pursue the Amalekites (1 Samuel 30:8). On his way to finding the women and children and confronting the Amalekites, David and his men came across an Egyptian man and were kind to him. They fed him and gave him water because he hadn't had any for three days – he was stranded.

After they took care of him, David inquired more about him and why he was out there. Turns out, he was the slave of an Amalekite man (1 Samuel 30:13). They had left him behind and clearly didn't care for him. Because of David's kindness, the man told him exactly where he could find the Amalekites. Talk about an extreme turn of events. David didn't have to stop for this man let alone be gracious to him. Because of his ability to be flexible in his journey, God used this man to get David right on track to his destiny.

If you aren't picking up what I'm putting down about the process of your journey, I just don't know what else will help you. You must be sensitive to the Holy Spirit's guidance and be obedient when he tells you to attend to different assignments for a little while. You never know when it might boomerang back to you in connecting you to your next thing. By now, you should be raising your hand when God asks who he can use to help someone in need. Allow yourself to expand and enlarge your territory and see how God will propel you into your destiny.

Prayer Time

Lord, simply help me not to miss Malta on my way to Rome. Help me to be obedient in the seeming inconveniences of life. I want to adopt to a lifestyle of flexibility and be attentive to the Holy Spirit's lead. In Jesus's name, I pray, amen.

Process of Here Activity:

Stop Blocking Your Miracle
Time: 1 week

Seeing how God chooses to get people from one place to another, it's important to not miss what you're supposed to do in this season that he may want to use in the next season. God tells you to do things through someone else, the written word, a sermon, or other vessel, and those instructions are confirmed by the spirit. It's when you know without a doubt that you are supposed to do something. Often, you might play this down as overthinking or try to suppress it so that it doesn't bother you. However, you know when you heard someone tell you something or a verse literally jumped off the page into your heart that the Lord spoke for you to move in a certain direction. This could be asking someone for forgiveness, taking a step to write a book, or even increase your giving to the church and others. Whatever it is, God has spoken.

Doubt, fear, comfort, and complacency plagues find themselves in your heart stopping you from obeying what God told you to do. Whether it seems practical or not, God requires you to move in obedience and faith to see Him do the things only he can do. When God promised to give us life and life more abundantly, it wouldn't come without our participation in the process. God is not a magician with magic tricks; he performs miracles. If you want to see the Lord move on your behalf in this journey to extraordinary purpose, you need to stop blocking your miracles.

Activity

Read the following stories in the Bible and list what God told individuals to do to see a miracle. Then think over your life and see if God has asked you to do anything that may be blocking your miracle.

John 11 (Story of Lazarus)
Exodus 14 (Story of Moses and the parting of the Red Sea)
John 5 (Story of lame man being healed)

What is God telling you to do or has told you to do that you haven't done yet? What is stopping you from doing it? What will you do to begin the process of doing what God told you to do?

Principles of Here

I want to provide you with some things to incorporate into your journey that will help keep you moving forward to your extraordinary purpose. These principles will challenge you to improve your stewardship capacities, stretch your discipline in consistency, and provide you with tools you'll need to maintain your spiritual walk during and after this initial walk through of this entire experience. When the Lord revealed these things to me, some I found to be easier to incorporate than others. However, I found that applying all of them helped me grow in ways I couldn't have imagined. I promise if you start to exercise these principles, you'll see the weight of your problems subside and your faith and endurance grow.

Let's start by talking about stewardship. This means that God has placed you over something for you to manage it for Him. All through scripture, you can see that God intended for people to use their time, talents, and treasures to expand his kingdom agenda here on earth. It started with Adam in the garden. Genesis 2:15 (CSB) says, "The LORD God took the man and placed him in the garden of Eden to work it and watch over it." Though the earth and all that's in it belongs to God, he uses humans to oversee, take care of, and govern all that is down here. God expects you and me to be good stewards of the things he has entrusted to us. Whether that is money, time, skills, or other things, you have a responsibility to be diligent in how these things are used. That brings me to my first principle for you to learn.

Principle One: Use What You Have

Many people think if they had more money, they would give more to others. They may believe that if they have a few more followers on social media, they will begin to start putting out the messaging for their business. I'm sure you have known people who receive something and still don't do anything they said they would do if they received it. If you're honest with yourself, you've probably been that person too. Listen, I'm the first person to admit that I've said one thing and done the opposite. If you are elevated to a new status, get a promotion, have more money, or whatever, it just usually brings out what is already inside of you. If you're not giving, serving, or investing now with what you have, then you won't do it when the next stage of development is ready for you. What do you have now that will help you prepare for the next level?

Two similar passages in the Bible (Matthew 25:14–30 and Luke 19:11–27) are often talked about in connection with stewardship. The ending reveals the same principle about how to bring value back to the master by managing well what he gave you. The differences in the stories are key for making this principle come alive. In one of the stories, the servants receive different amounts of the items and in the other they receive the same amount. People are all given three categories of possessions to steward over (which I mentioned earlier): time, talents, and treasures. However, people aren't all given the same amount of these things. Some individuals will pass away sooner than others. Some are wealthy and have a lot of material items while others don't. Some have many talents and abilities that other people might not possess. Nevertheless, there was still an expectation that each servant does something great with what he had been given.

That's why I'm challenging you to begin with what you have. If you feel God has called you to do something, begin to take a step of faith by using what he's already given you to do what he asked you to do. Remember that God likes to see faith in action before he does his part in the situation. This could be increasing your commitment to tithing and offering in the church. You might be asked to spend more time volunteering with a ministry or organization when you've never done it before. God might have you write a book so people can read about your personal journey and learn from it (speaking to myself here). Whatever it is, start with what you have to do what God has called you to do. In one of the activities in this section, I'll help you determine what you have and how God might want you to use that expand his kingdom agenda.

In these parables of the servants, the master gave the faithful stewards more to steward over. That's how God operates with you too. In Matthew 25:23 (CSB) God tells you, "his master said to him, 'Well done, good and faithful servant! You were faithful over a few things; I will put you in charge of many things. Share your master's joy.'" When God sees that you have been a blessing to others and not withheld what he gave you to be beneficial for others, he will reward you with more. Rest in the confidence that God will provide for you as you continue to work with what he gave you. He is aware of what he has already given you. Be faithful with what seems little and watch how God can make it big.

Let me be frank. Being able to control your tongue and what you say is a challenge. I would be lying if I said I'm perfect at this. Though I've been convicted to be better in this area, it took me a while to practice and be consistent in how I use my words. This goes beyond using curse words or profanity. It also includes gossiping, lying, crude humor and jokes, negative put-downs against others, false accusations, and even denying God's power. You have to learn to be intentional and not careless with your words. This extends to social media as well. Learning about the need to control what, when, and how you say something will change the trajectory of your life. The Bible is full of passages that talk about the importance of watching what you say. I want to go over a few that I think will help start you off in the right direction as you move to your extraordinary purpose.

Proverbs 18:21 (CSB) states, "Death and life are in the power of the tongue, and those who love it will eat its fruit." Take a second to think about that for a minute. Life and death can be impacted based on the words that come out of your mouth. Talk about powerful imagery! The most powerful reference to words used in such a manner is in Genesis 1 when God spoke the universe and all there was into existence. Being made in the *imago Dei* (image of God), your words can also be used to see such magnificent things take place. This doesn't mean you can just say things and then they will appear. You are not a magician or God, so it doesn't work like that. What this is referencing is the effect your words can have on a particular situation. You may negatively or positively affect someone or something based on how you speak about it.

I'm sure you can remember a bully from your childhood or something a parent said that stayed with you forever. It could have been something about how smart you are or perhaps how you don't have any worth. People like to say, "Sticks and stones may break my bones but words will never hurt me." However, that couldn't be further from the truth. Words can heal, help, or hurt. One day, you and I will be held accountable for every idle word we say, text, or post (Matthew 12:36). Think about that when you use your words.

Additionally, Mark 11:23 (CSB) says, "Truly I tell you, if anyone says to this mountain, 'Be lifted up and thrown into the sea, and does not doubt in his heart, but believes that what he says will happen, it will be done for him.'" Ultimately, what you say will have an impact on many areas of your life. You may be dealing with an area that has been difficult to overcome, such as sexual discipline, lust, greed, or overindulgence, but nothing you tried seems to help you be strong. What Mark 11:23 tells you is that, as a follower of Christ, you can literally make these big issues in your life not have power over you anymore. Those tough circumstances and things you want to see removed from your life can be by speaking it and using the authority and power that God gave you to make them move.

Lastly, something I encourage you to do when watching what you say is to use your words to testify to God's goodness. Others need to hear how God has been working in your life and circumstances. That's the way you bring others into the fold. You can't be stingy with keeping Jesus only to yourself or to other believers. By speaking about what you have been through or are going through, you will see others be inspired, healed, convicted, and changed. By your words, you can live victoriously. When you speak about the things God has done for you, you remind yourself of the truth of his power. You can overcome Satan and his minions by proclaiming with your words the works of God in your life.

Practically speaking, you should always be slow to speak and quick to listen. I'm sure you've heard people say the reason you have two ears and one mouth is because you should be listening twice as much as you speak. Not every situation calls for you to get something off your chest or to speak your opinion. You may need time to gather your thoughts before you say something or not say anything at all. Learn to start filtering what comes from your mouth and see how God impacts not only your life but the lives of those around you.

Principle Three: Don't Overthink

As the self-declared president of the Overthinkers United Club, I can assure you that you have to train your mind, which is a hard thing to do. When you start to hear more specific directions from God, you can find yourself being caught up in overthinking. As he reveals more of his plan for your life, you might end up teetering into thoughts about how it's going to happen, what the result will be, what the purpose is, and more. Overthinking can cause you to become overwhelmed and doubtful in God and stop you from being prepared for your extraordinary purpose.

At the heart of it, I believe overthinking comes from a lack of faith. When you start to look at your situation instead of the one who can handle it, it's easy to find yourself in a paralyzing situation. If you aren't careful, you can think yourself out of a miracle that God wants to do in your life. Martha and Mary almost missed out on the opportunity for Jesus to raise their brother Lazarus from the dead because of their overthinking (reference John 11). Faith doesn't always have to make sense to our human minds. That's why God tells us in Philippians 4:8–9 (CSB), "Finally brothers and sisters, whatever is true, whatever is honorable, whatever is just, whatever is pure, whatever is lovely, whatever is commendable—if there is any more excellence and if there is anything praiseworthy—dwell on these things. Do what you have learned and received and heard from me, and seen in me, and the God of peace will be with you."

When you focus on these healthy things, peace will start to overcome you. However, the more you constantly think about why something won't go as you planned or all the negativity that is happening because of a situation, you will struggle to keep going. You have to keep looking at God who has brought you from your past to where you are now. Even if it's not where you want to be in the end, you have to think about how you even got *here* in the first place. Any new day on this earth is another day for your extraordinary purpose to get to you.

Dr. Charles Stanley, pastor of First Baptist Church in Atlanta and president of In Touch Ministries, provides a list that you can utilize if you find yourself overthinking something. Address these questions and see if you can move forward in your thought process.

- Where will these thoughts lead me?
- Will these thoughts get me where I want to go?
- Are these thoughts scripturally acceptable?
- Will these thoughts build me up or tear me down?
- Could I share these thoughts with someone else?
- Where did these thoughts originate?[1]

If you see that the answers to these questions show that your thoughts are not where they should be, then you need to take them captive and cast them down (2 Corinthians 10:5). That's a very churchy way of saying, "Take hold of the negative thoughts and remove them from your mind." When you remove them, you must make sure you fill that space with something else. What you fill it with should be God's words and truth. If you don't replace it with something healthy, you leave room for negativity to creep back in. You must control your thoughts and make sure you think with God's truth as your foundation.

Principle Four: Be Flexible

I've felt the need to reiterate this principle even though it was mentioned in the chapter called "Process of Here." Paul and Jesus as two prime examples of embracing the flexibility of side projects while building to their extraordinary purposes. Approaching life in this manner can work in your favor. There is nothing wrong with having a routine and being comfortable in what you expect your day to look like, but your routine has to allow for flexibility. Speaking from experience, routines can cause you to be rigid and miss opportunities because you lack being guided to do something different.

---

[1] Stanley, Charles. "Taking Control of Our Thoughts."

As you build prayer into your daily routine, God will give you directions on what to follow. This could be something as simple as paying for someone else's coffee order or waiting to go to the postal office until after work. If you aren't flexible and willing to follow God's lead throughout the day, you can potentially miss out on the very encounter he was going to use to bring you to your extraordinary purpose.

I know you might be thinking that God isn't that specific or doesn't speak that clearly to you, but I can guarantee that he does. When you build that communication with him, you can ask him about decisions on everything you do during the day. The God who knows every hair on your head also cares about every move that you make. Once I discovered that I can ask God about my schedule for the day, I started doing just that. God will answer about what seem like small tasks and the greater ones too. He operates off timing. That's why it's important to keep Him in the midst of everything you do.

Psalms 37:23 (CSB) says, "A person's steps are established by the LORD, and he takes pleasure in his way." God will give you peace or confidence about what he called you to do. The more you obey what he has told you, the more he will be able to trust you with bigger tasks. If you are flexible, you can start to appreciate life's "inconveniences." I'm still working on this if I'm being honest, but I'm starting to truly experience God at a more intimate level by working on flexibility. High traffic or a wrong food order can tempt you to become angry or upset. However, in those seemingly random inconveniences, God might bring about the encounter that will bring your extraordinary purpose to you.

I don't want you to not plan for things because you think God is just all willy-nilly. However, I want you to make sure that you aren't boxing God out of doing something in your life because you are too rigid. That's the beauty in life. If life were full of the same ole, same ole, you wouldn't be fulfilled. Let God show you more about him by seeing randomness as something to embrace.

Principle Five: Give

I am fully aware that you might shut down when you hear the word "give" in any form associated with God, the Christian faith, or the church. Your mind quickly tries to defend why you should not and would never give to the church. I'll admit that there have been terrible representatives of faith both nominally and practically. However, I encourage you to sit with what I'm going to share about giving and allow yourself to digest this principle.

Let me first break down the lie that giving is all about money. Giving can come in the form of emotional support, a listening ear, a shoulder to cry on, or a meal to be cooked. You might overlook all the other facets of giving and negate what God wants to do in your life when you selflessly give. I want to present to you two Bible passages that teach about giving and why you should apply them to whatever season of development you are in for your extraordinary purpose.

Luke 6:38 (CSB) states, "Give, and it will be given to you; a good measure—pressed down, shaken together, and running over—will be poured into your lap. For with the measure you use, it will be measured back to you." The key word in that verse is *it*. There is no specificity when it comes to what you can give that will be given back to you. If you give out love, you will receive love. You can give out encouragement, and you will receive it back. This is awesome news. If you need something, give it out first and watch how it boomerangs back to you.

The important thing to note is that the word *it* can even be negative. If you put out unforgiveness, that's what you will receive back. If you put out disrespect, you will get that back. I know society would have you believe in the concept of karma, but that's not what it is. God made this principle so that even if you don't believe in Him, you will still see results from it. It's called the principle of sowing and reaping. Galatians 6:7 (CSB) says, "Don't be deceived: God is not mocked. For whatever a person sows he will also reap."

The giving and sowing principle essentially has the same outcome. When you put a seed or a few seeds in soil, you will always grow more than the amount you planted. There should be no surprises in what you receive back because you should expect that apple trees come from apples, so the seed is important to what you get. With that expectation, I hope you are cautious about how you interact with people. The only way to stop the manifestation of what you've planted is to get to the root and pull it out. That's a lot more work than putting the right seeds in the ground ahead of time.

I hope this has opened your thoughts about giving and that you are beginning to think differently about what you give and what you sow. If you need friendship, go be a friend to someone else in need. If you need financial blessings, be willing to give from your finances. It's not a magic trick to try to hold God hostage to doing what you want Him to do, but it does allow Him the opportunity to bless you in your time of need. Consider the story of Paul in Malta again. He gave to the people generously and in return, they gave to him exactly what he needed for his purpose. What you are willing to give out in kindness and generosity will come back to you more than what you ever gave out. You never know when something you're giving to will be the thing God uses to bring your extraordinary purpose to you.

Principle Six: Faith-Filled Community

I have witnessed so many people struggle with this principle of community. You might even be thinking, "I already have friends, so I'm good to go." What I'm about to share will have you reevaluating your current circle and it might make you uncomfortable. It might require you to end certain relationships or it might require you find connections with people who aren't typically who you would be around. As you go deeper into your relationship with God and walk out your faith, there will be natural drifts from people who can't keep coming with you in your journey. This is a sad reality that I faced. Though most of these non-faith connections didn't end on bad terms, there was a natural drift because I was getting closer to God and further from my old habits and ways of thinking.

Good community is so important in making it through this life that God showed us in two different methods how important it is. Genesis 1:26 (CSB) says, "Then God said, 'Let us make man in our image, according to our likeness.'" This verse points to multiple people having a discussion by the usage of the word *our*. Though not explicitly stated here, this refers to the Holy Trinity composed of God the father, God the son (Jesus), and God the Holy Spirit. From the beginning, God has always existed within community. Additionally, in the gospels of Matthew, Mark, Luke, and John, you will notice that Jesus spent life during his ministry years with a group of twelve disciples. If God operated within the context of community, how much more important do you think it is for you to be in a good community?

Don't just take my word for it though. Let me point you to two passages that discuss what having a good community can do for you. Proverbs 27:17 (NIV) is a well-known verse, and it reads, "As iron sharpens iron, so one person sharpens another." I bet you've had friends before who complained all the time, or always had something negative to say, and that would affect your whole mood. People feel so hopeless in today's culture that they can't help but be negative about everything. How many times have you been on social media and the constant Debbie downers ruin your mood? That's what happens when you don't have the right kind of community around you. You will become an Eeyore before you know it if you don't have people around you who are encouraging and uplifting.

Moreover, you need a faith-filled community to help you be strengthened in this life. Ecclesiastes 4:9–12 (NIV) states, "Two are better than one, because they have a good return for their labor: If either of them falls down, one can help the other up. But pity anyone who falls and has no one to help them up. Also, if two lie down together, they will keep warm. But how can one keep warm alone? Though one may be overpowered, two can defend themselves. A cord of three strands is not quickly broken." You need people on whom you can rely in tough times. You are guaranteed to be in trials and tests in life, so who can you depend on when you're going through something? You want people around who can comfort you while also not taking offense to any change in emotions you have in those low seasons.

If you don't have people in your corner who you can get in the weeds about life with, you need to change your inner circle. This is a tough choice to make, but it's so worth it. At this moment, I challenge you to find some accountability friends who can talk about your journey with you. Ask God to reveal to you who might not be good for you to connect with right now and then obey when he tells you who you need to cut. I'm not saying you have to be rude when you disconnect from people. You should still do it with love and kindness if you have to have a conversation about it. Though it may be difficult to go through, the results of it will be unimaginably better than you could think. I encourage you to read the story about a faith-filled community and how it changed the life of one of their friends in Mark 2:1–12. Then write out your thoughts regarding this story.

Now it's time for the wrap-up. I know this was a lot of content to consider and think about all at once. However, I believe that when you research these topics in the Bible, you will notice the importance God places on these principles to help you be sanctified and set apart for this life. You are supposed to reflect the life of Jesus to others. If you start to examine how you can improve in these areas of your life, I'm sure you will start to notice how it not only affects you but others around you. These principles help people to identify you more with the faith and help you shine brighter in a culture that is dark. Please use the following workbook activities to guide you through more discussion about these principles and see how God might raise your standards in certain areas of your life.

Prayer Time

Lord, I ask that you help me incorporate these principles in my life. Help me to have an increased standard of holiness and to follow you. I pray you show me how to be better in all areas of my life so that I can see you work powerfully through me. In Jesus's name I pray, amen.

Principles of Here Activity 1:

Stewardship Responsibilities
Time: 2 weeks

Now that you've been given some principles to incorporate into your life, I want you to dig deeper on these topics. You may use some of the information in each principle as a starting point. As you study these over the next couple of weeks, I want you to pray over each category and see how God directs you to raise your standards of holiness.

Instructions

Use the list below and pray over each category. According to scripture, what does God say regarding the topic? Check whether you are rising to God's standard in this area. If not, write out how you will make changes to reach his standard. In the blank rows, write out other areas that you've thought about that God has given you to steward over.

Category	What does the Bible say about this topic?	Are you meeting the standard?	How will you reach God's standards?
Finances			
Giving			
Your mouth			
Friendships			
Serving			
Possessions			
Physical Health			
Spiritual Life			
Church			
Entertainment Options			
Career			

Thought and Ideas

In the spaces below, write additional thoughts, questions, or ideas that God has given you through discovering how you can better steward over the responsibilities you have in your life.

_____

_____

_____

_____

_____

_____

_____

_____

_____

Principles of Here Activity 2:

Gratitude and Praise
Time: 1 week

A tactic to maximizing your current season and remaining positive is the act of practicing gratitude and praise. Over the next two weeks, you will spend time intentionally acknowledging the things you are grateful for in prayer and in praise. The goal of this activity is to keep you focused on the daily provisions that God gives you to move you from *here* to *there*. If God sustains you in the ordinary, you can expect Him to sustain you in the extraordinary. In a spirit of gratefulness, God deserves to receive all your praise.

Believe it or not, sometimes praise will bring you to your breakthrough. Read how Paul and Silas used praise to literally break physical chains that were meant to keep them bound in Acts 16. Use this activity throughout your journey and see how it impacts you.

Create a Gratitude List

Take some time to reflect on the things you may have forgotten that are sustaining you from day to day. There are times when you may be so focused on your future that you don't soak up all God has done to even keep you alive, protected, and well today. Matthew 6:34 (CSB) says, "Therefore do not worry about tomorrow, for tomorrow will worry about itself. Each day has enough trouble of its own." There are some categories to get you started on your gratitude list, but feel free to add your own. After you make your list, pray and thank God for the things you may have taken for granted or just expected God to do for you. Then take time to pray to Him for increased trust in Him to be able to sustain and bring you to your destiny as you continue to maximize your current season.

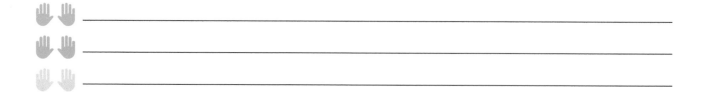

Create a Praise Playlist

The Bible mentions repeatedly how God loves to receive our praises (e.g. Psalm 22:3, Psalm 70:4). Through praise, you can experience breakthroughs (see Acts 16). Even in difficult seasons of life, there is still much to be thankful for. When you are emotionally drained, you still must praise. There will be times when you have to give a sacrifice of praise (Hebrews 13:15) when you may not feel like praising, but you do it anyway because God deserves it. It's in those moments, like when Paul and Silas were in prison yet praising, that you see the power of God revealed.

Over the next two weeks, tune into your playlist each day to give God praise. You can utilize your time in the car, in between work meetings, while you work, during your devotion time, and so on. The time that you can praise is endless. Try to increase the amount of time you praise each day by one song.

4

Pace of Here

Welcome back! I hope your fast was as life transforming as it was for me. At any point in this journey, I support you in partnering activities together as you go through more of them. As mentioned in the introduction, this is not meant to be a checklist of activities. It is meant to help you experience God more fully to move from ordinary living to extraordinary purpose. Therefore, you are encouraged and supported to work through the activities at your own pace.

Speaking of pace, that's the perfect segue into the topic for this next part of your journey. Previously I mentioned that you are in control of you fast you move from the valley to the mountain. What this comes down to is how badly you want to do it. For example, let's take you back to elementary school days when kids had to run a mile in gym class. There was always the kid who wanted to finish the activity so he or she could have open gym activities for the rest of class. The kid came ready to run and put forth great effort to finish. Then there were the kids who started strong, but then became bored or tired and started to jog. They still finished but didn't have as much open gym time as the sprinter. Then, there was always the group of kids who decided they would just walk the mile instead of attempting to run. Lastly, there was always the complainer who didn't bring gym clothes, proper shoes, or a good attitude and received an F for the day. Which child are you going to be on this journey?

Even though I have enjoyed the valley for how it has refined me and shaped me for my destiny (which is how this book even came to be), it wasn't always like this. I was determined to get to the mountain as quickly as I could. I didn't know how far I would have to go, which is something only God knew, but I understood I was going to play my part in doing the hard work to get there. After it was revealed to me the things God didn't like in me, I went all out in finding resources such as sermons, books, and podcasts to help me in those areas of development. As I mentioned, I didn't know how to give up self-sufficiency or idolatry, so I had to tackle them in bite-size pieces. Similarly, things you have discovered about yourself may confuse you and make you wonder what you should do next. You want to get rid of these things since God doesn't like them, but you just don't know how. Don't be discouraged if that is you. This is a process of literally allowing God to do the transforming and cleaning as you do what you can. If you have a sincere heart in wanting to follow Jesus and to be changed, he will answer your prayers for that growth and development.

Simultaneously, I had to not only give up those things God didn't like, but I needed Him to help me with a renewed faith. Hebrews 11:1 (CSB) states, "Now faith is the reality of what is hoped for, the proof of what is not seen." If you're like me, you can understand how difficult it can be to instill confidence in something you can't see. Though I've known God for most of my life, I never had to experience this heaviness of life by myself. This was new territory for me, and it was scary to extend more trust and faith in God. I never doubted his character as the almighty savior and creator, but I did doubt his care for my situations and his desire and ability to turn my ordinary life into extraordinary purpose. Yet, in my fast-paced sprint to the mountain, God changed that around for me.

Romans 10:17 (NASB) says, "So faith comes from hearing, and hearing by the word of Christ." This is exactly how I was able to tackle a good leg of the journey quickly by dealing with bitterness, unforgiveness, and my faith problems. I didn't realize that, through my attempt to be studious about my journey, I would consequently end up with solutions to my problems. At this time in my life, I cut out a lot of the noise that would have been antagonistic to any progress I would make. Therefore, I limited television time, time hanging out with friends, YouTube videos with bad advice, and so on. The risk and sacrifice of these was less important to me than the greater good that could potentially result from doing them.

With limited entertainment and increased spiritual and knowledge development, I didn't realize I was set in motion to start seeing some good changes occur. I literally felt the healing take place from my sadness about my dad's passing to feeling more joy and hope for what life had in store for me. I wasn't going to be defined by the mistakes or failures I made in the past, but I was determined to finish my race in this life stronger than how I started. By this point, I'm hoping that you are starting to feel invigorated to keep going in this valley of life. I don't want you to stop short because of the scariness, cold nights, and length of the valley, because you never know when you'll finally reach the base of the mountain.

I would be remiss if I didn't connect my life experience with a story from the Bible that ties directly into the concept of pace. Most people who have any level of familiarity with Christianity know the infamous story about Moses and the Red Sea. Mainstream entertainment was so fascinated by this event that they've made movies about it like *Prince of Egypt*. As with that movie, most of the story is often only told to the point where the people of Israel escape Pharaoh and his troops through this supernatural move of God. Applause and fireworks are often the resounding noise when the story is stopped there. However, the story takes a turn for the worse after that.

You see, God delivered the people of Israel from Egypt and promised to give them a land flowing with milk and honey. That's the direction they were headed after the Red Sea event took place. Deuteronomy 1:2–3 (CSB) tells us, "It is an eleven-day journey from Horeb to Kadesh-barnea by way of Mount Seir. In the fortieth year, in the eleventh month, on the first day of the month, Moses told the Israelites everything the LORD had commanded him to say to them." Whoa, Nellie! How in the world was the trip the people were supposed to take to this Promised Land only eleven days, but they are still being talked to in the fortieth year? The book of Exodus that lays out the details that followed the parting of the Red Sea. The Israelites had a lot of growth and development to achieve before they would make it out of the wilderness and on to the Promised Land. Through constant complaining and grumbling, the people were taking their sweet time in the wilderness, moving from the valley to the mountain. They were that kid I mentioned who earned an F in gym class for the day. Because of their refusal to keep it going, God ended up revoking this conditional promise and made it so that only their children twenty and under would receive the promise of extraordinary living.

Hindsight is always twenty-twenty and that's what makes this process challenging. None of us knows how far away the mountain will be and are prone to giving up on the course because of that. When you already feel defeated, deflated, and hopeless, it's hard to want to take a risk of faith to keep going. You can find yourself becoming comfortable in the valley the longer you choose to stay there. That can eventually lead you to settling for the monotony of what you know versus what could potentially be out there.

I'm sure if the people of Israel knew that their breakthrough was just a little bit away, then they would have had the ability to keep going. However, that's not faith, and unfortunately God's currency is faith. He wants to see you trust Him before he shows out. It can be scary to release the control and to fully surrender in all areas of your life. However, when the source of what you trust in has a great track record of success then you can be more confident in continuing to press forward. That's what helped me keep my pace up as well. Like I stated, I didn't know that deciding to cut out entertainment and fill up my mind and spirit with helpful tools would move me along to overcoming obstacles faster than I anticipated. My faith moved God to do what he needed to do. When that happened, it gave me more energy to keep running. It was like running a 10k where I felt tired but then saw my friends waving at me from the sidelines and encouraging me to finish; I was instantly more energized and strengthened to speed up. God was not only cheering me on, but he was and is running with me. I finally felt lighter and freer. I knew I was on the right path for God to turn my ordinary living to extraordinary purpose and to change my external situations around.

This too can be your reality. I want you to know I'm cheering for you during this race. You may not know the distance you have to go, and I can't promise it's only going to be an eleven-day journey. I can promise that God will renew your strength as you keep trusting and putting in the work. Every day you take the time to grow, the closer you are to the valley being done. Be here and continue to do the work.

Prayer Time

Lord, I thank you for being my biggest cheerleader and running the race right beside me. Help me to have the wisdom to tackle these issues that I know are not up to your standard. I will continue to move at a pace that shows my dedication and seriousness for change. Guide me to my finish line. In Jesus's name, I pray, amen.

Pace of Here Activity:

Inventory and Implement
Time: 2–3 weeks

When you're in a valley, it is important for you to release the things that are going to slow you down during your journey. You have a say in how quickly you get to the mountain. Some of the things you will have to give up you will be able to get back when you get to the other side; some things you will have to give up permanently. It's important for you to think about what God is molding you for and what won't be helpful for you to have as you go. This could be relationships (friendships, family, or romantic), entertainment options that don't put you in a good mindset, social media time or following negative influences, and so on.

Write out how you currently spend most of your weekdays and your weekends. Be detailed in your schedule. If you aren't sure what your days look like, take a week to be attentive to your schedule and write it down.

Monday   Tuesday   Wednesday   Thursday

Friday   Saturday   Sunday

Look at your schedule for your average weekdays and weekends and mark off where you have wasted time. Cross off things that will interfere with your personal growth and development. Place the list of items that you will be removing during this journey in the space below and write a statement of commitment to laying these down for the betterment of yourself.

_____

_____

_____

Now that you've taken time to release the items that won't be helpful for you, you should replace them with things that will help you increase your pace. Taking ownership of your spiritual growth and development will speed up the pace of development that God desires of you. List resources that you can use to help aid in your growth. If you are stuck, here is a list of resources I used during my journey.

Books

- *Kingdom Woman* by Chrystal Evans Hurst
- *Fervent* by Priscilla Shirer
- *Kingdom Disciple: Heaven's Representatives on Earth* by Tony Evans
- *Kingdom Stewardship* by Tony Evans
- *Experiencing God* by Henry Blackaby
- *Resilient Hope* by Christine Caine
- *Power of God's Names* by Tony Evans

Podcasts and Media Content

- Dear Future Wifey
- The Basement
- 30 Minutes with the Perrys
- Trinity Broadcasting Network (TBN) YouTube clips

Groups

Ministry opportunities at church

Friends in their spiritual walks

Hosting group events at home

Over the next month, track how these resources have started to challenge old thoughts, attitudes, and behaviors. To see growth, you must implement the things you are reading about and listening to in your life. As you change old ways, reflect on the questions below. In your prayer journal, write down your responses to these questions.

- Where in my life has God challenged me to increase my spiritual activity?
- What is difficult about changing old behaviors?
- How have the development resources helped cultivate more Christ like actions in my life?
- Has God communicated any more revelations to me about my circumstances?
- How has God begun to stir up a direction for my destiny and extraordinary purpose?

Patience of Here

Patience is the p-word that I'm sure nobody wants to talk about. Truth be told, most of you have heard about the necessity of patience forever. If you have been thoroughly churched in life, you've probably heard the metaphor repeatedly that says, "Jesus is not a microwave God – he is a crockpot God." In layperson's terms, that means that he likes to take his time with how he chooses to complete the work in our lives. Most people, like me, struggle with patience because we want things done now. We want to be healed now. We want the miracles now, but that is almost never how God works. That's why I must talk more in detail about patience, how to increase it, and how to use it to your advantage in this season.

The best way to combat hastiness or trying to move too fast is to be present-minded. If you can fix your mind on the things you need to do today and really embrace where you are *here*, you'll be able to increase your patience. It takes intentional following of God each day to be patient. One of the greatest examples of what it looks like while moving from ordinary living to extraordinary purpose, or here to there, comes back to the people of Israel that I talked about earlier in the book.

When these people were moving from the Red Sea to the Promised Land, God guided them daily through two practical signs: a pillar of fire and a cloud. First mentioned in Exodus 13:21–22 but explained more thoroughly in Numbers 9:15–23, God guided the Israelites through the movement of a cloud during the day and a pillar of fire at night. When the cloud stayed above the tabernacle, the people would stay in the camp. When it started to move, they would immediately pack up and follow it until it settled again. The passage in Numbers 9:20–22 (CSB) states, "Sometimes the cloud remained over the tabernacle for only a few days. They would camp at the Lord's command and set out at the Lord's command. Sometimes the cloud remained only from evening until morning; when the cloud lifted in the morning, they set out. Or if it remained a day and a night, they moved when the cloud lifted. Whether it was two days, a month, or longer, the Israelites camped and did not set out as long as the cloud stayed over the tabernacle."

This is honestly one of the best depictions of how God operates to move you from *here* to *there*. Ludacris would later receive recognition for this method by rapping, "When I move you move—just like that!" However, God was the OG of such an operational tactic. The people had to acquire patience while on the route to the Promised Land. There were times when the Lord would move them a couple days at a time or a month at a time closer to their destiny. I'm sure that's probably what God has been doing with your journey as well. I experienced this as I went through this process.

At times God would expedite me toward my destiny and extraordinary purpose, and I would juggle doubt, exhaustion, and excitement. The doubt was from seeing myself moving forward and then seeing God telling me to halt and stay camped for a while. This made me think either I had misheard God or wasn't doing things properly. The exhaustion came from being given multiple unexpected tasks, sometimes quicker than others, and needing to ask for more grace to accomplish things. The excitement was because I knew I was moving forward on the promises God had for me. All these emotions simultaneously presented themselves repeatedly as I walked through this journey. However, I know that God was taking me through the valley little by little to preserve my destiny and ensure I would be strong enough to continue to get there. He will similarly do that for you.

Two important factors helped the Israelites with this patience walk that will apply to you as well. They had to keep God in their presence to lead them, but also, they had to obey immediately and follow where God was headed. As I mentioned, some of us become so excited about what lies ahead of us that we end up being hasty and move ahead of Him. Then some of us either become discouraged, tired, or stubborn and don't move when he is ready for us to move. Both scenarios are terrible positions to be in and can have negative impacts on the patience needed to keep at the pace that God wants you to go. You must submit to God daily to see if it's time to move, and if it's not, then you must be patient and steward well over what he has told you to do. I'll talk more about stewardship in the next chapter. Then when it's time to move, you must not waste time getting on with the next leg of the journey. God is purposeful when it comes to why he may direct you to go and stop, and it will be important for you to learn the dance of patience if you don't want to step out of God's will.

I've come to realize that the amount of focus I put on today's tasks helps strengthen my patience. I wake up daily and ask God specifically for two things each day: to be guided by his wisdom and to do what he has called me to do for the day. While I have other prayer requests, I always ask God for my daily provision of guidance and wisdom. When I meditate on his words for me throughout the day and continue my constant conversations with Him, I find myself being less anxious and accomplishing more than I could have imagined. I wake up more energized and ready to tackle the next day ahead of me. I do what I'm set out to do (which is typically to work), and then I leave room for God to guide me to do other tasks as well. Some days he has had me meet with individuals who need some encouragement and love. Other times he will give me an opportunity to help someone on my lunch break, and there will be moments when he gives me an idea or dream for my future.

Allowing myself to focus on today, though I do plan for tomorrow, keeps me sane and peaceful. The peace and patience often goes together as you surrender to God to lead you to wherever he wants you to go. During this process, there were times when I would become frustrated and discouraged. I had to remind myself that God was moving me to my destiny little by little. Those days, I would cry and pray for more grace, and to see Him give me a little wink or sign that said he was working and had me right where he wanted me. Each time that would happen, God showed up and always got me through the day and sustained me to keep going forward.

Fortunately, I can look to the scriptures to build my faith and study how others exhibited patience to help encourage me to continue to push forward. David had great patience. After being anointed, returning to his position as a sheep boy, serving Saul with his lyre-playing skills, and defeating Goliath, he still wasn't moved into his extraordinary purpose. David had to deal with Saul's jealousy of him and trying to hunt and kill him multiple times, and David's willingness to spare his life. When Saul finally died, David was promoted as King of Judah. It was nearly fifteen years between the time David was anointed and fulfilled that role. When there is a higher calling on your life, you will have to go through many seasons of development, which will require much patience.

If I had been David, I would have been frustrated to know that I was supposed to do something great, but it didn't seem like it was going to happen. Before he ultimately became king, David was able to get married, establish an alliance with Saul's son Jonathan, and have some other victories. It wasn't like good things weren't happening, but the thing he knew he was purposed to do didn't fully present itself for a while.

That is like the patience Joseph exhibited while he waited for his extraordinary purpose. After being thrown into a pit and sold into slavery, his master's wife tried to sleep with him, but he refused to do it. She lied and had him thrown into prison. While there, he was still in a position of favor and trust. He interpreted the dreams of two other prisoners who served Pharaoh. When the one prisoner was released, Joseph told him to remember him so he too could be released. This individual forgot until two years later when Pharaoh had a dream that needed to be interpreted. Joseph was able to interpret the dream and became second in command over Egypt. It was thirteen years before Joseph was finally pushed into his destiny. Along the way, he stayed connected to God with faith and patience.

Each new season is a new opportunity to grow and learn. Some valleys and journeys will require more patience than others. Therefore, you have to look to God to keep you strong or you might be tempted to throw in the towel too soon. God likes to see faith in action. That's why he doesn't give you the plans. He gives you enough to get to the next step to see if you will do what he already told you to do. Then he can trust you to move on to some more. If you feel that God has told you something, keep holding on to that no matter what anyone else says.

It's also important to realize that as these two men demonstrated great patience, they didn't complain. They just kept showing up to what they had in front of them and were extremely present and diligent. While waiting for their own situations to turn around, they continued to serve others. Neither Joseph nor David withheld being kind to others and being used to advance people even though they knew they had something great for their lives. They were very unlike the Israelites who never reached the Promised Land because they kept complaining and wouldn't move forward.

I have a personal story to share about patience and how it resulted in the fulfillment of dreams. God is so intentional that he established a desire in me to move to Texas in college. I don't know when it officially became my dream to live there, but I remember telling all my friends in college that I was going to live there one day. At the time, I knew this is where I was supposed to be even though I had never been there before. By the time I reached college, the farthest I had been was Costa Rica for a mission trip in high school. Other than that, I stayed within a 3.5 hour radius from my hometown in Beloit, Wisconsin. Nevertheless, I just sensed that Texas had more to offer me than I currently had experienced.

I attempted to go to Texas after I graduated from college by applying to two graduate schools there. My decision to pursue a different degree type steered me in a new direction for school choices. I figured I would willingly go to graduate school for public health for two years and would find myself in Texas quickly after that. If I survived undergraduate for four years, it would be quick to complete two years and be done. I enjoyed my time in South Carolina completing my master's degree, but I didn't want to settle there after graduating without having ever tried Texas. I knew I had to see what that state had to offer.

As graduate school was wrapping up and I needed to choose where I wanted to work, I sent my application to many places in Texas. None of these applications received any attention. God brought me to Mississippi instead after graduate school, which ended up being my last stop before Texas. During my time in Mississippi, I experienced a lot.

I was able to develop the work that was being done around wellness. If you check out their current work, you can see that many of the things I created are still in continuation. Somewhere in the six-month mark, after I had officially moved to Mississippi, I decided I would start to spend some time with my coworkers outside of work. The only issue that I had was that they were either graduate students or people with families, not people who were in the same stage of life. Many weekends I would find myself at my grandparents' house. I would run from the town of Oxford as much as I could to be anywhere but where God had me. My soul wasn't at rest there because I continued to wrestle with the fact that I was living in Mississippi.

Honestly, I was frustrated with God because he brought me to Podunk Mississippi (as I called it then). He wasn't allowing me to really have community, wasn't bringing a good man, and I didn't have any activities to occupy my time or so I thought. I felt overworked, underpaid, and overlooked. I smiled a lot on the outside, but I was struggling with my placement and purpose. After the first year there, I decided that I would try to move to Texas. Surely, being in Mississippi with all these struggles wasn't what God truly wanted for my life, right? I started casting nets far and wide. Houston, San Antonio, Austin, and Dallas were all places I considered living in Texas. I didn't research any of the places. I just figured any place would be better than Mississippi. I knew I was more than qualified for any of the jobs I applied for, but God shut those doors and made sure I stayed put in Mississippi.

A little after my second full year of being in Mississippi, I started to feel that I wanted to maybe consider trying to move to Texas again. It happened after my parents went to Dallas for their birthday, holiday, and wedding anniversary festivities in December 2018. They explained how much they loved visiting the city and all the exciting adventures they had during their time there. I'm my parents' unofficial travel planner, so I booked the flights, hotel, and rental car for their time there. I was vicariously living through them while they lived out my dream for a week.

Being mad and upset about this desire to try and move to Texas again, I dug my heels in and decided I wasn't going to be looking or applying for jobs. I figured God wanted me in Mississippi, so I was going to stay there—forever. However, work became challenging. I was starting to feel tension from a student employee of mine and from my supervisor. I am all about correction and want to receive feedback and critique about how to improve my work or leadership style. However, I could tell I was receiving unjust reviews. That was the icing on the cake, just enough for me to start looking and actively applying for jobs in Texas. You know, God will use anything to work for our good, and this just so happened to be the spark I needed to get searching.

This time, I wasn't casting a wide net hoping that just anyone would accept me. I was looking at salary, the city of Dallas only, jobs that would elevate my skill set, and other well-intentioned things I wanted in my next move.

When I'm telling you God made this process super quick and convenient, I mean just that. The turnaround time from starting to look for a new job, interviewing, accepting the position, and choosing a start date was no longer than five months. God was ready to bring this dream to fruition. The sad part is that honestly, I was unworthy of even seeing this dream fulfilled because I was disobedient and not walking in God's purpose intentionally for a while. However, I do know the character of God. He will use the good, the bad, the ugly, and the ordinary experiences to accomplish his will for your life and in the bigger picture of his agenda.

Before I finished my time there, a new assistant vice chancellor was hired. This was my boss' boss' boss. She came to one of our department meetings to meet the staff. Knowing I was on my way out soon, I was just showed up to do the minimum to make it through the day. All those "get to know each other" meetings are usually very boring to me. I used to think I didn't stand out much, so I introduced myself quickly and wait for the next person. The new assistant vice chancellor told me in front of everyone, "I just want you to know that your reputation precedes you. I've heard great things about the work you do on this campus, so I just wanted to let you know that it hasn't gone unnoticed." My heart was literally shocked as the whole room stared at me, probably thinking I was the most unlikely person to receive such a compliment. Even though I was on my way out, God made sure to publicly acknowledge me before it happened.

As I reflect on that story now, I can clearly see how God made intersections, changed my heart's desires to be in alignment for what he wanted for my life, and ultimately got me where I needed to be. All I had to do was show up each day and do what he told me to do next. The thoughts came seemingly out of nowhere. That's how God operates. One day you are doing one thing, and in a moment, God brings someone, something, or some thought to your mind that changes everything. That's how I began to write a book. God is still working out the next part of my extraordinary purpose too. It doesn't stop here. He answered that prayer at the appropriate time. I wouldn't have had the appreciation for Texas and would still probably be searching for something unattainable if he didn't do it in the right time. I had to work through a lot of patience in that season, and I'm only really having an appreciation for that now. I'm so grateful for God to have taught me that. Every day you wake up is another day to take a step forward by continuing to be here.

Prayer Time

Lord, I pray that you increase my patience. I know this is a tough prayer to pray, but I trust you will strengthen me in the journey to my extraordinary purpose. Help me not to grow weary in my walk and to take it one step at a time. In Jesus's name I pray, amen.

Patience of Here Activity 1:

Seeds and Harvest
Time: Planting 1 hour, Watching 1 year

One of the things that helped me tremendously with patience during my journey to extraordinary purpose was planting. Having been a millennial parent of plants (a.k.a. plant mom) for many years, I found the connection between caring for plants and the patience needed to see the manifestation of what I had sown. Often in the Bible, God uses the theme of sowing and harvesting to impart lessons and principles to us. This activity will be helpful during your time of waiting to encourage you to keep going when you feel like nothing may be happening.

Materials Needed:

Soil
Seeds
Pot

Take your materials, and research what type of soil, water, and sunlight your seed needs to be successful. Different seeds need different care packages. Once you have that figured out, care for your seed as much or as little as needed with sunlight and water. Over the course of your study and journey, write down your observations of the plant. Use some prompts below to help you monitor what's happening in the physical and connect it with your spiritual growth.

Month 1

- Have you seen any changes in your life because of your engagement with this material?
- What steps did you take to plant your seed that were like your partnership with God in moving from ordinary living to extraordinary purpose?

Month 3

- Are there any visible results from your plant? If so, what are you seeing and how does that relate to your walk with Christ?

Month 6

- Have you experienced any challenges with your plant and sustaining it? If so, what are they?
- Do you have any discouragement or difficulties with your growth and development that relate to the development of your plant?
- Is your plant growing slower than you anticipated or are you happy with its results?

Month 9

- List any emotions, observations, or thoughts concerning the taking care of a plant.

1 year

- Where is your plant now? Is it bigger than you anticipated?
- What growth have you seen in your life this year?
- What connections can you make between your plant and your spiritual growth and development?

Tips and Tricks

1. If this is your first plant, try obtaining something that is low maintenance and can be kept indoors. You don't want to be discouraged by accidentally taking care of something beyond your skill level.
2. Don't watch the plant daily. Time is necessary for growth. The plant will begin to sprout and then it will appear to stall in development. That is normal and is often the case with our spiritual lives as well. You may not see constant growth from week to week, but the consistency will show a lot.
3. Expect more than you planted. This is just like your spiritual life. Your seed may be small, but it will always produce something greater than you anticipated.

Patience of Here Activity 2:

Rest and Relaxation
Time: 1 month

This is one of the simplest yet most complex activities to walk through. Take this entire month to do nothing but maintain. Don't add anything to your plate in responsibilities (unless guided by the Lord). When it comes to spending your time, don't stretch yourself beyond what God has already given you to steward over. There are times when you need to just stop so that you do not become burned out on your journey. Follow the example Jesus laid before us. He fulfilled everything he was supposed to do on this earth in three years without burning himself out. You too can appreciate the rest and casual movement in your journey to your destiny. Write down your thoughts and emotions regarding rest this month below. Use the following prompts if you are stuck on where to begin.

- What does resting do for my emotions?
- Do I find myself being in my head a lot more while I'm resting?
- Has God revealed anything to me in this month of rest?

_____

_____

_____

_____

_____

_____

Promise of Here

By now, my hope is that God has been speaking to you and that you have been able to recognize his voice more. I know this journey has required a lot from you emotionally, physically, and spiritually and you might need some motivation and encouragement. As you may remember, Jeremiah 29:11 tells you that God's plans for your life are to give you a future and a hope. That is one of the greatest promises that you can reference when it comes to your spiritual walk with God. Thankfully, the Bible is filled with other promises like this one and I want you to embrace them to see powerful changes take place in your life.

You and I are so fortunate to live in a time when we have the complete canonized scriptures available for us to read. I couldn't imagine having to walk by faith like people who were in the Bible, but especially those in the Old Testament who didn't have any written words to follow. I want you to use the written word to your advantage for letting God speak to you about the things that he has already promised to do in your life.

I did a quick Google search of the definition of a promise, and this is what it says: "A declaration or assurance that one will do a particular thing or that a particular thing will happen."[2] How awesome and extremely kind of God to declare and assure that something will happen for you? The problem is that God has already promised to do so many things, but people are unaware of his words, so the promises go unclaimed. A promise is no good if you don't have the knowledge about it which will give you an expectation for it to take place.

God has given you authority to piggyback on the power of Jesus by being a disciple of Him. Because of that, you can experience God in ways that are personal, powerful, and life changing. Through his words, God wants you to hold Him accountable for the things that line up with his will. When you have a challenge in your life, you can turn to God and remind Him of what he spoke in the Bible as a means of claiming a promise over

---

[2] Dictionary.com, 2012.

your situation. I've found this to be one of the most effective ways to pray. When I see there is a scripture that relates to my circumstances, I boldly come to God and tell Him, "You said!" For a little razzle dazzle, I always throw in the connection with Jesus because I know that anything the Son asks on my behalf will be done.

You too should operate like this when it comes to claiming a promise in the Bible. Having taken this journey, I began to see more prayers answered when I started praying in this manner. I realized that through my repentance, dedication to obeying, and doing all I knew to do, God would then start letting me see bigger prayers being answered. James 5:16 (CSB) states, "The prayer of a righteous person is very powerful in its effect." At this point in your experience, you should be able to confidently go to God and pray his words back to Him regarding these promises.

The only precaution I want to share is that you can't rush God on when to fulfill a promise to you. In Genesis, Abram (later known as Abraham) and Sarai (later known as Sarah), were given a promise from God that they would have a child. Because it had taken longer than they wanted or expected, Sarai concocted a plan that would interfere with what God had already promised them. Instead of trusting that God would be faithful to do what he told them he was going to do, they tried to make their own solution to the promise. I've been known to do that myself a time or two, or three, or—who's counting?

If God promised that he was going to do something for you, I want you to stand firm on that word. With Sarah and Abraham's story, I don't know if God would have brought Isaac sooner if they wouldn't have interfered. I do know that their hastiness caused an entire mess. You need to be careful not to use your own limited knowledge to make a promise come to pass.

I know that possessing a promise for yourself can be tough. You should believe and expect that it will happen for you. If you are still having trouble trusting that a promise is something from God and not just something you made up in your head, I want you to go through these questions that Dr. Charles Stanley came up with and see if you can answer yes to them.

- Is it consistent with the word of God?
- Is this a wise decision?
- Can I confidently ask God to enable me to do this?
- Do I have the witness of the Spirit?
- Does this fit who I am as a child of God?

- Does this fit God's overall plan for my life?
- Will this honor God?[3]

God is such a gracious and kind God and wants to do a lot for your life. Take his words seriously and hold Him to it. Let God's promises keep you from falling. Stand strong in what he has said and watch Him go above and beyond what you could have even imagined.

Prayer Time

Lord, I ask that you help me take your promises to heart. I trust that you will be faithful to keep your word. In Jesus's name I pray, amen.

---

[3] Stanley, Charles. "How to be Sure of God's Will."

Promise of Here Activity:

Claiming Your Promises
Time: 2 weeks

Did you know the Bible is filled with endless promises that God makes for those who are followers of Him? These include things such as taking all things that happen to you, by you, or against you and working them together for good, or the promise to be the head and not the tail. If you have been churched for a while, I'm sure you've heard many verses or partial verses at some point in your life. Whether they were from an old church mother or an old-school pastor, these verses may have just seemed like religious rhetoric. The activity that you are about to participate in will challenge you in the areas of scripture memorization and promise integration in your life. Here's what you'll need to complete the activity.

Material Needed:

Notecards
Colorful pens/markers
Bible Scriptures

Instructions

1. Find three verses that speak encouraging promises about your life (e.g., Jeremiah 29:11, Ephesians 3:20). You may need to use the verse finders in the back of your Bible or do a web search on certain verses on specific topics.
2. Once you have your three verses, write each verse on a separate notecard.
3. Place the promises around your house in areas that you frequent (e.g., bathroom mirror).
4. Over the next two weeks, recite these verses as you come across them in your home.
5. Throughout the two weeks, read the entire chapter or book where the verses are.

6. In the section below, write what has been revealed to you by reading the chapters/books where the verses are located.
7. Pray a specific prayer to God to help you take hold of the promises for your life and to grow you in faith to receive the promises.
8. Write out any specific dreams you have and see if they pass the question test listed in the chapter.

Bible reading revelations and thoughts

Write your thoughts and revelations from reading and praying about your promises.

7

Power of Here

You've made it—at least for now! I hope that by the time you've reached this point in the book, you've seen some of the greatest changes, both internally and externally, that have propelled you forward to your extraordinary purpose. I wish I could tell you that, by this point, if you completed every activity intentionally and really took ownership over your spiritual development, you would be exactly in the middle of your destiny, but I can't promise that. However, what I know to be true is that you should be in God's will and walking more righteously, which is the secret to unlocking all that he has for your life. James 5:16 (NASB) tells you, "The effective prayer of a righteous man can accomplish much." Therefore, since you have turned around to living at a standard that is pleasing to God, you can go before Him confidently and watch how he shows up to answer the prayers you have asked Him about.

While you wait for God to intervene on your circumstances, I encourage you to stay the course and stay anchored to Jesus. Some answers to prayers will come quickly and others God will take his sweet time with delivering a response. However, in this season, I pray that you take the lessons you have learned during these past few months and continue to show up every day and ask God, "What do you want me to accomplish today?" Staying focused on the present will help you continue to walk the path set before you to get you where you're supposed to be in life.

Now that you've gone through this journey, I want to challenge you to find someone else you can pass this information to and perhaps walk in the experience with them. The goal is to continue to elevate others to this standard. Then everyone can experience God doing the impossible by partnering with us to bring his kingdom agenda down to earth. There is so much God can accomplish when people have allowed Him to lead them from ordinary living to extraordinary purpose. It's time to play your part in being a blessing to someone else in discipleship and watching how God continues to trust you with more as you do what he has called you to do.

Be prepared for this cycle to continue as you move through life. Trials and tests are guaranteed to come. James 1:2 (CSB) states, "Consider it a great joy, my brothers and sisters, whenever you experience various trials, because you know that the testing of your faith produces endurance." When those trials hit, you can come back to this process, bringing yourself back to the basics, and walk through it again with more peace and greater expecation. Start from the beginning to see what God is trying to build in you as you walk through another valley and preparing to climb another mountain of success. The next time you walk through another valley, you'll be stronger and better equipped to face whatever comes your way.

It's now time to say goodbye to each other and for you to be the leader in someone else's life. Continue to follow the cross and you'll end up exactly where you need to be. While you are waiting to get *there*, the time to enjoy life is always *here* and now.

Prayer Time

Lord, I thank you for this journey through the valley that has changed me from the inside out. You have brought me through life thus far, and I will continue to trust you as you walk with me the rest of the way. Help me to be the light in someone else's story as that person follows you to get where he or she needs to be. In Jesus's name I pray, amen.

Power of Here Activity:

Reflect
Time: 1 week

It's a time to reflect and journal your thoughts. This is important because you need to be aware of where you are emotionally and spiritually so that God can keep stretching, challenging, and changing you from the inside out to prepare you for your extraordinary purpose. Use some of the prompts below to aid in writing if needed.

- Are you still holding on to the promises God has spoken to you?
- Has God revealed anything else to you? If so, what are those things?
- What is the stretching process like for you? Have you grown fatigued?
- Have you followed God obediently and immediately in everything he has asked you to do?
- What challenges are you experiencing?
- What surprising positive things have been taking place in your life and in your heart?

ACKNOWLEDGMENTS

The cornerstone of my life is Jesus. Thank you for allowing me to be used by you to advance your kingdom work. Thank you for making yourself real to my grandma, Linda, who passed the faith down to my daddy. Thank you for the union between my parents (that means you too, mommy) to raise their children and grandchildren in the faith. To my friends Namoonga, Kelsey, Brianna, and Danielle, you all have been wonderful accountability partners in this walk of faith. Lord, if you don't do anything else for me, you've already done too much. Thank you, and I am forever grateful.

Author Biography

Taja T. Hereford loves to lead people through personal experiences and seeks to break down the stereotypes related to being "churchy." She has a background in public speaking, group discipleship, and church volunteer service. Through her writing, she hopes to encourage, challenge, and uplift others to dedicate their lives to living as a true disciple of Jesus Christ.

Printed in the United States
by Baker & Taylor Publisher Services